Embracing Community

LIVING AN INSPIRED LIFE

ROBERT E. WAGNER

Embracing Community: Living an Inspired Life
Robert E. Wagner
Wild Sacredness, LLC
Ashland, Oregon
www.wildsacredness.com

© 2016 Wild Sacredness, LLC.

ISBN: 978-0-9863114-5-1

Second Edition

Printed in the United States of America
10 9 8 7 6 5 4 3 2

For the courageous men and women who are committed to bringing forth their unique gifts for the benefit of their people and the world.

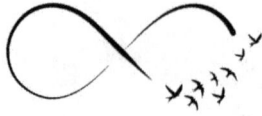

"Don't ask yourself what the world needs. Ask yourself what makes you come alive and then go do that. Because what the world needs is people who have come alive."

~ Howard Thurman

Introduction

"**N**O MAN IS AN ISLAND" wrote the poet John Donne back in the 1600s...but the phrase rings even truer today, when the world is shrinking in so many ways and people and nations are so intricately linked—economically, socially (through electronic media), climate-wise, politically. Many are genuinely concerned about what's happening on the other side of the world, as well as in their own backyards...and often a sense of helplessness pervades. So often at the later stages of a person's life—and now frequently even earlier—you hear them say, "I just want to feel I've made a difference."

Of course, meaningful engagement always starts with self, and then extends to one's community. Wild Sacredness is committed to facilitating active engagement with our brothers and sisters, through tools that enable individuals to realize their unique passion, purpose and power, support one another as they grow, and materialize the steps to bring their gifts forth to their communities.

You could imagine concentric circles: we have our immediate families, relatives, colleagues at work, close friends. The next circle of relationships is our community—the co-housing unit, or suburb, town, or city that we live, work and play in. As we grow, it's natural to want to give back in appreciation for opportunities we've been given, and to nourish our locales so that future generations may thrive. As we become clearer about what we have to offer, and gain the personal empowerment to manifest that through the tools of Wildness Within and Sacred Desire, the real fulfillment begins. We embrace community.

You'll step into authentic living and begin to give your gifts...and those gifts matter. At a certain point, you can't hold back—you just *have* to share the treasure you've discovered inside, welling up from your authentic, vibrant self. And everyone gains. Your stepping out, even into unknown territory at first, liberates others to do the same, and 'community' becomes a dynamic celebration of shared energies and exciting accomplishments. Together we can solve problems we couldn't dream of tackling on our own. And best of all, we have the reciprocal positive feedback loop that keeps us all growing, striving, and enjoying the journey together.

The following exercises in *Embracing Community* offer a glimpse of how we can bring forth our gifts and share them effectively in our surroundings—creating an impact we might never have imagined!

THE EXERCISES

"IF YOU CAN'T FIGURE OUT YOUR
PURPOSE, FIGURE OUT YOUR PASSION.
FOR YOUR PASSION WILL LEAD YOU
RIGHT INTO YOUR PURPOSE."

~ BISHOP T.D. JAKES

Clarifying Your Life Purpose

WHAT IS YOUR LIFE PURPOSE? What are your gifts? This exercise will help you to articulate your unique mission.

Depending on where you are in your life's journey, you may already have realized your life purpose. And you may have been giving your gifts to your people for some time now. That's wonderful! However, if you're unclear about your personal vision—what you feel you came here to accomplish—or if you've been holding back from sharing that, then keep reading.

If you can't recognize your mission, what's standing in the way of your seeing it? Some fear? If you've been holding back, is it because you feel it's not the right time to give your gifts or possibly you feel your gifts aren't good enough for the world? With desire and appropriate tools, these obstacles can be removed.

I believe that every man and woman is innately blessed with unique gifts meant to be shared with others. Author John Powell has written:

"You have a unique message to deliver, a unique song to sing, a unique act of love to bestow. This message, this song, and this act of love have been entrusted exclusively to the one and only you."

One of Wild Sacredness' most powerful offerings for getting clear on your life purpose is the Sacred Vision Quest. It's a rare opportunity to dive deep within and reconnect with your 'wild self,' your essence, that intuitively knows what you came here to do. If fears have kept you from recognizing and owning your gifts, the quest empowers you to embrace them and begin to bring them out to the world.

But until you decide it's time to go on the quest, this exercise will start you on that 'soul excavation.' In the early stages, your life purpose may just be an idea, a resonance with some activity or environment, or a quiet whisper hinting at what you want to manifest. So it's important to listen closely and hold that sweet whisper (it may be faint) very closely, cherishing and nurturing it as if it were a delicate seed. The goal is to eventually have it clearly articulated, so you have a firm foundation from which you can begin to build.

- You can start with a "Day Walk," a walking journey outlined in *Wildness Within*. The Day Walk, or "Medicine Walk" as it's known in native traditions, is a chance to declare an intention, such as gaining clarity on your life purpose, and receive messages from the natural world in response to it.

- For an additional, more sedentary exercise, begin with journaling about your idea or that faint voice that's been beckoning (quietly, maybe) for years. I recommend doing this in a place where you feel expansive and have minimal distractions. Start giving it form and expression through words. It helps to just keep writing, without letting your pen stop, and without censoring anything you've written. You might start with a sentence such as "What I've always wanted to do in my life is...." and write out different ways to complete that sentence, one after the other. Or "When I'm most fulfilled, I am ..." Or "What I came here on earth to do is...." Just don't stop the pen, even when you might be writing something unrelated...your thoughts will soon come around to focus on the topic, just be patient. You'll know you're on the right track when you feel some excitement and have a sense of being a bit more 'alive'. Don't worry about the wording or proper grammar. Just let your thoughts, ideas, and desires flow out onto the paper or the computer screen.

◆ Another angle to approach to pinpoint your mission is to ask yourself:

What do I love to do? What am I passionate about? What makes me feel most alive? Your mission lies within your answers to these three questions.

You may have always wanted to be a professional writer and publish a book about your work or your adventures. A doctor or teacher? Perhaps a musician who creates a touring band? Or a social entrepreneur? A fabulous father or mother? Possibly you've dreamed of sailing around the world, researching some aspect of science, designing and building your own home, or becoming an environmental activist? The possibilities are endless, and fortunately, uniquely yours.

◆ Now try closing your eyes and visualizing what exactly you're doing when you have that feeling inside of "This is the real me. This is what thrills me, what makes me feel connected and joyous." Feel free to invite the opinions of others who know you well—they may see something rather obvious, that for various reasons you've kept hidden.

By all means, be as grandiose and outrageous as you like. This is not the time to think small or to question if it's even possible. After you feel you've captured a sense of your life purpose, then begin to polish the raw words into a precious, finely crafted gem—one that reflects your unique gift to the world.

"UNTIL ONE IS COMMITTED, THERE IS HESITANCY...THE MOMENT ONE DEFINITELY COMMITS ONESELF, THEN PROVIDENCE MOVES TOO. A WHOLE STREAM OF EVENTS ISSUES FROM THE DECISION...UNFORESEEN INCIDENTS, MEETINGS AND MATERIAL ASSISTANCE, WHICH NO MAN COULD HAVE DREAMT WOULD HAVE COME HIS WAY. WHATEVER YOU CAN DO, OR DREAM YOU CAN DO, BEGIN IT. BOLDNESS HAS GENIUS, POWER, AND MAGIC IN IT."

~ WILLIAM H. MURRAY

Keeping Your Vision Alive

K EEPING THE VISION FOR YOUR LIFE WORK alive is essential or else it may slip away. However, I've found that if it's truly your life purpose it will eventually return again and again. Spirit won't let you sidestep your path too long. And why would you want to? Life is too short to spend your time doing anything else but your heart's true mission.

Therefore, to keep your dream alive you must hold onto it in your awareness. Consider it a precious seed that only you can nurture. And remember, the more attention you consistently put on your goal, the more it can feed you—supplying the energy you'll need to execute your action steps.

* A good way to keep your vision lively in your awareness is to write it down and place it on your mirror, refrigerator, or your

special place—your 'altar', if you will, that holds a sacred space for your intentions and commitments. Create a vision book or board filled with photos, words, thoughts, and anything that will inspire you about your life purpose. Post it in your bedroom or at your desk at work. It's also helpful to create a manifesting journal for keeping track of your thoughts and ideas on how to transform this dream into reality. The point is to become emotionally and energetically connected with it.

- Remember that you are connected to Spirit, and when you listen to your inner guidance you can trust the universe to give you what you want—if your energy vibration matches your level of thought. When you're most truly alive, you're aligned with the tremendous energy which brought you into existence and which wants to help bring forth your gifts. So try to keep your *dominant thoughts and beliefs* matching the *expansiveness* of your vision, and not fall back into thinking that LIMITS your potential as a creator—thoughts like 'My gifts aren't significant,' or 'I don't have the energy to do this.' If you keep your thinking focused on what you want to create, the law of attraction will support manifestation of that. When you go with the strong stream of what inspires you, it will feel wonderful—nothing can hold you back. So as you keep asking for manifestation of your vision, Spirit will match the vibration of that desire and propel you forward, if you keep yourself energetically aligned with your vision.

- Devote an hour once a day or a few hours once a week to focus exclusively on your life purpose. Make this time an official part of your schedule, and choose someone to be accountable to, to make sure it happens. Spend this time exploring, researching and developing your purpose and how best to bring your unique gift to your people. The discipline required to commit to this time will serve you well down the road as you begin to activate your goal—it's an essential part of 'reconditioning" yourself, creating new habits so that your ideas will actually germinate.

◆ Consider your vision to be in gestation. You need to nurture and protect it in its early stages of development. Especially be careful not to share your vision with others too soon. This is very important because one friend's critical comment can easily cause you to question the value or importance of your vision. And that's not what you need at this stage.

◆ This exercise honors the value of quieting the mind, for rejuvenation and inspiration. Make a commitment to yourself to put aside time each day to nourish yourself in stillness. If you already have a meditation practice, be consistent with it in your daily routine. Take time out to BE and to feel whatever comes up in the quietness. In other words, take time away from consciously focusing on your mission—step back to gain a broader perspective, the big picture. Opening up to a larger field of possibilities, the expansive field at the source of your ideas where all change comes from, will speed up the changes you've called into your life that accompany manifesting your vision. Contacting a field of broader awareness may give you new, clearer perspective on just where you want to go with your vision.

◆ "Timing is everything" is a well-known phrase. There will be a time to share your vision with those you trust. By giving voice to your vision, it will help you clarify and hone your purpose. And your friend may be able to mirror back your purpose or share some perspective that opens up other possibilities or refreshing insights.

◆ Start to take active steps in exploring and experiencing your life's purpose. If you've always wanted to be a writer, join a writer's club. If you're a poet, participate in poetry readings. And if you've always wanted to design and build your own home, then spend time at the drawing board or on your computer making the floor plans. Possibly, visit a few job sites to see how various contractors operate in the construction process.

◆ You can't always just think and write about your life's purpose. The time inevitably comes for you to step outside your comfort zone and begin to taste your dream. Try it on, and make sure it fits. If necessary, you may discover that you have to learn certain skills or develop special talents to bring more success in manifesting your purpose. But don't get defeated, these are just more opportunities to recommit.

———— ••⟨∞⟩•• ————

There will be times when you question yourself and your purpose. That's to be expected when you venture into uncharted territories. But don't lose faith. It may just be time to revisit your original intention or spend some time with a trusted friend and share your doubts and concerns. I always consider these challenges as invitations to go deeper with my commitment to my purpose. Trust me, it's not always going to be easy, but once you've attained a certain level of stability those few questionable clouds will be long gone.

So foster your vision with all the creative energy you can muster. Make it your daily practice, and continue walking through any fires of doubt. Before you know it, you'll be ready to take the next step of offering your vision to the world.

Living Your Life Purpose

S O YOU'VE CLARIFIED YOUR LIFE'S MISSION, and spent adequate time exploring and experiencing it. Now you're ready to offer your gift to the world—let's make it happen!

This exercise will focus on practical steps for manifesting your specified goal, so that you can begin LIVING your purpose every day.

◆ Create an ACTION PLAN. What are you going to DO, so your vision becomes actualized? You'll need to outline each step you'll need to take to make your dream happen, whether it's meeting with someone who's already doing what you want to do and learning from them, or setting up a free 'session' to give people a taste of your gift, or gathering the pieces you'll need to present the gift, like writing your first children's story, etc. You may need props (or a new wardrobe!), or contacts, or finished products...or you might even need to take a class to acquire the particular skills needed to actualize your mission. Whatever the step is, a big or a small one, WRITE IT DOWN. It needs to be formally stated and acknowledged before it's going to happen. If it helps to work backwards, try this:

◆ Picture yourself actually giving your gift. What do you look like? Who is there with you and how are they receiving it? What is the venue? Then work backwards, and you'll see what needs to happen, and in which order. For example, when I realized I dearly wanted to share the healing and enlivening power of Tantra with my community, I started by offering free lectures on human sexuality at local colleges. Not only did it give me a picture of what people are looking for in intimate relationships, it allowed me to practice sharing my knowledge in a public forum. I learned how to fine-tune my message to match what my clients were ready to hear. It gave me confidence in my presentation skills and refined my understanding of how best to share this knowledge. It prompted me to return to my Toastmasters group, to maximize my public speaking ability. The positive response from these presentations encouraged me to take the next step, presenting workshops for a fee. Now I'm giving sessions on "A Taste of Tantra" at a local community venue, getting paid for my offerings and making contacts that further build my business. I have continued to expand my offerings and create these booklets to invite people in to Wild Sacredness. Again, start simple, with something not too out-of-reach. The success naturally follows from there.

◆ Make a chart for yourself, starting with where you want to be in five years, or one year...whatever increment you want to begin with. Delineate exactly where you will be in progressing toward your goal, and that will help you break the big project into concrete, achievable steps. A mansion isn't built all at once, but one stone at a time. Your life purpose evolves in stages, as quoted by William Murray at the start of Exercise 2; you'll begin to receive support from your surroundings as you move forward.

◆ Find a person or group to whom you can be accountable, to ensure that taking the action steps actually happens. These days you may find a support group for people in the process of changing careers, or wanting to start a project—and who want others they can meet with to stay on track with their goals. It could also be a close friend, someone willing to meet with you maybe weekly to hear about your progress, and to suggest helpful ways to be more productive if you're not meeting your targets. Accountability is very important so we don't delude ourselves that something is happening when it isn't...or that something will happen automatically without your taking the necessary steps.

◆ Make time in your schedule to TAKE the STEPS you've outlined. This time should be as carefully guarded as taking time for meals or brushing your teeth. Even if it's only 10-15 minutes each day, take it seriously. Remember, if you're serious about creating the life you want, you've got to be serious about taking the steps that will get you there.

◆ Another valuable point: Be open to how Spirit will support you. Don't assume or expect it to look or be in a certain way. Be open to all possibilities. Then you won't miss the magic when it appears.

◆ Celebrate your achievement of the little steps! These daily actions will gradually and sometimes imperceptibly transform into big, wondrous accomplishments. You will have gone from a vision to a living, breathing reality. You'll be part of an exciting, regenerative energy as your contributions enliven your community, which in turn will feed future achievements, and on and on. Best of all, you'll experience the fulfillment of dynamic engagement with those you care about, through manifesting the gifts that you came here expressly to give. Well done!

"YOUR TIME IS LIMITED, SO DON'T WASTE IT LIVING SOMEONE ELSE'S LIFE AND DON'T LET THE NOISE OF OTHERS' OPINIONS DROWN OUT YOUR OWN INNER VOICE. MOST IMPORTANT, HAVE THE COURAGE TO FOLLOW YOUR HEART AND INTUITION. THEY SOMEHOW ALREADY KNOW WHAT YOU TRULY WANT TO BECOME."

~ STEVE JOBS

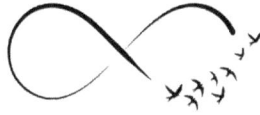

IF YOU'VE FOUND THE INFORMATION in this booklet helpful and inspiring, then we invite you to learn more at: **www. wildsacredness.com**. Click on the "Embracing Community" offering to learn more about manifesting your gifts and sharing them with your people.

If these exercises have sparked you to go deeper, give Robert a call at 541-201-3411 or email robert@wildsacredness.com. He offers a **FREE "Clarify Your Life Purpose" session**—where you can share your results from the exercises one-on-one with a qualified guide, and learn how the tools of Wild Sacredness can keep your momentum going to create a rich, empowered life. The session will:

1. Create a sense of clarity and direction about your life purpose.

2. Uncover the essential building blocks for living your mission.

3. Discover the #1 thing stopping you from bringing forth your gifts.

4. Identify the actions that will help you achieve what you desire.

5. Show you EXACTLY what to do next to discover and live the meaningful life you truly want!

Robert is also available to give educational presentations and lively experiential workshops on clarifying your life purpose, keeping it alive, and living it for yourself and your community.

Wild Sacredness is dedicated to bringing forth the authentic, passionate essence within each of us, and nurturing that as we manifest our individual power and purpose, our capacity for deep, intimate relationships, and a dynamic, engaged relationship with our community.

Robert E. Wagner
Founder and Director, Wild Sacredness

WILD SACREDNESS is the outgrowth of the inner and outer journeying Robert has been doing for most of his life. As an Eagle Scout and member of the Order of the Arrow, he spent his first time alone in the wilderness as a young teen. Soon after that, he began his practice of Transcendental Meditation and spent many years living and studying in a prominent spiritual community.

In 1996, Robert participated in his first vision quest; he has continued to use the quest as a tool for empowerment and self-awareness, going on a vision quest every year. The discovery of Tantra as a vehicle for profound healing and fulfillment fit perfectly into Robert's array of tools for embracing one's wild, sacred, sensual presence and sharing that with others. As a member of the Mankind New Warrior Project and creator of men's empowerment groups, he has honed skills as a personal development facilitator and community builder.

In addition to his qualifications as a professional wilderness guide, certified Tantra educator and group facilitator, Robert brings 35 years of success in the corporate world as a marketing executive and multi-craft technician. He is also the father of a daughter in her thirties.

A compassionate and gifted communicator, Robert approaches people with deep respect and intuitive wisdom. He has developed an uncommon ability to create a safe, sacred space supporting profound transformation for individuals, respectful of their unique personal paths and pace of growth.

For a full listing of Robert's credentials, visit
www.wildsacredness.com

The exercises contained within this booklet build on the transformation that results from the Wild Sacredness offerings— in this case, the clarity of vision and personal empowerment that participants gain from going on the Sacred Vision Quest. Read on to see what men and women are saying about how this profound journey has enabled them to embrace their true calling and create avenues to share that with their communities.

"Getting beyond my fears and accessing my own power on the quest, I was able to ask myself, 'What do I really want?' It's been magic ever since, watching my healing practice gain more momentum. I feel like I'm riding on an unstoppable energy guided by Spirit."

~ CARRIE M., MOTHER – CONCORD, CA

"The quest helped with a challenging transition from being a life-long student to a working professional. Through the healing and self-exploration, I now feel grounded, confident, and ready to make an impact through my teaching and counseling work".

~ SAM M., PROFESSOR – BERKELEY, CA

"I went on the quest because I felt I'd been living 'small' in my life, and I knew it was time to live 'big.' I needed a kick in the pants. I came back with a renewed sense of my purpose, and that what I do in life matters. I'm ready now to show up in my life and do what I came to do."

~ ELIZABETH H., TV PRODUCER – NEW YORK CITY, NY

"Approaching my 50th birthday, I was at rock bottom in my life— on the verge of divorce, unhappy in my work, financially ruined. I went on the Sacred Vision Quest to see if I could claw myself out of the hole. It absolutely transformed me, setting me up for an entirely different, successful life."

~ BOB K., FATHER – BOULDER, CO

"At a time when I sought healing for a deep emotional wound, the Sacred Vision Quest restored the meaning and purpose of my life. I gained trust in my healing process, my career passion was renewed, and I gained a sweet peace around watching my future unfold".

~ MARINA R., PROFESSOR – BERKELEY, CA

"Experiencing the silence, the natural elements and my own buried emotions on the quest has played a pivotal role in my life—in my marriage, in my vocational life, and in my well-being as an adult. I went on the quest at a crisis point in my journey. It is not possible to put a price on something that so effectively transformed me."

~ PETER S., RETIRED – LAS VEGAS, NV

"I approached the vision quest with curiosity, not knowing what to expect...I decided on a whim to take the plunge. It turned out to be absolutely one of the most extraordinary experiences of my life."

~ GREG D., BUSINESS OWNER – HEBRON, KY

"If anything at all is holding you back in your life from becoming who you really want to be, I recommend this quest."

~ SETH K., ENTREPRENEUR – BOULDER, CO

"I'm in transition from middle age to elderhood, and I wanted to become more conscious about how my life plays out for the years that remain to me. Robert encouraged me to look at the wisdom I've gained in my life, and reclaiming this was a major thing I took away from the vision quest. Plus the courage to share my gift with other people. I definitely got what I came looking for."

~ JOHN D., RETIRED – TACOMA, WA

"By taking the rare opportunity to look inward amid Nature's silence, I received some profound insight into my capabilities and power as a man. I learned that I'm far more capable than I had previously thought."

~ MERRILL W., MEDIA CONSULTANT – ASHLAND, OR

"The Sacred Vision Quest allowed me to dive within and discover the truth of who I really am. Now I can find my own answers by listening to Spirit and following her guidance. Robert is a master at this work."

~ BRIAN B., CRESTONE, CO

"I went on the quest to learn to speak my truth. As a result, I feel closer to my passion and it's been a real energizer for the new business I'm creating."

~ TOM G., ENTREPRENEUR – CALGARY, ALBERTA CANADA

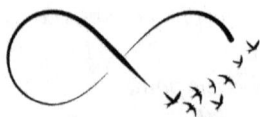

Other books by Robert E. Wagner in the Wild Sacredness
Series, available at www.amazon.com (print or Kindle eBook
format):

***WILDNESS WITHIN: Experience the Power of Your
Authentic Self***
A journey of exploration into your most prized possession—
your unique, wonderful self and the many gifts you have to
offer.

SACRED DESIRE: Secrets to Kindling Profound Passion
A journey into the unlimited reservoir of erotic energy and
sensual pleasure that we all possess.

08132016

www.ingramcontent.com/pod-product-compliance
Lightning Source LLC
Chambersburg PA
CBHW060549030426

42337CB00021B/4512